The Planets

The Solar System

Contents

©2016
Book Life
King's Lynn
Norfolk PE30 4LS

ISBN: 978-1-910512-84-5

Written by:
Gemma McMullen
Edited by:
Harriet Brundle
Designed by:
Drue Rintoul
Ian McMullen

A catalogue record for this book
is available from the British Library.

Words in **bold** can be found in the glossary on page 24.

The Solar System

The Solar System is the Sun and all of the objects that orbit, or go around, it. Eight planets orbit the Sun, including our home, Earth.

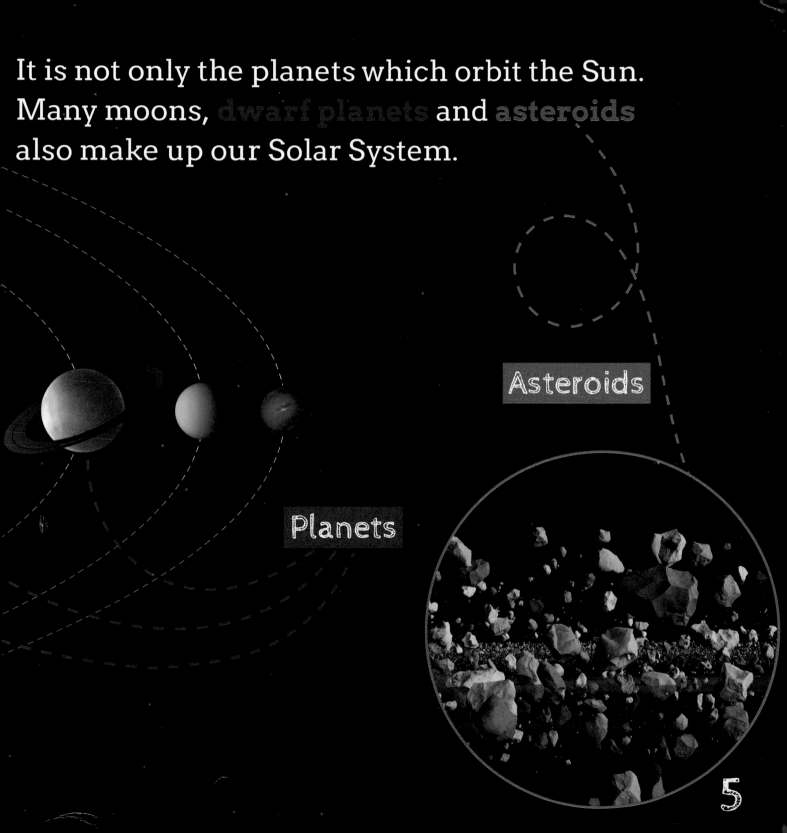

It is not only the planets which orbit the Sun.
Many moons, dwarf planets and asteroids
also make up our Solar System.

Asteroids

Planets

5

What are the Planets?

The planets are the largest objects to orbit the Sun. They are made from rock or gas. The names of the planets are Mercury, Venus, Earth, Mars, Jupiter, Saturn, Uranus and Neptune.

Earth

Mercury

Venus

Each of the planets has its
own orbit path so that they
never bump into each other.
They are each a different
distance from the Sun.

Earth

Earth is the planet that we live on.
It is made of rock. Most of Earth is
covered in water which makes it look blue.
Earth is the only planet known to have life on it.

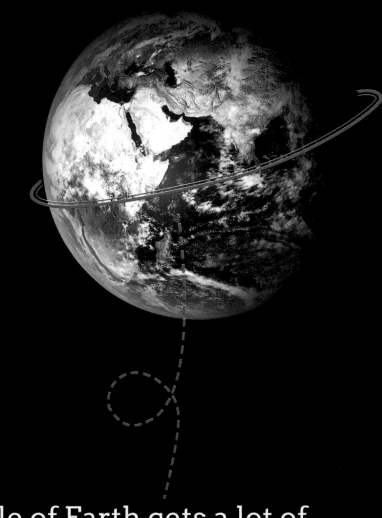

The middle of Earth gets a lot of sunlight so it is the warmest part of the planet. It is called the Equator.

9

Mercury and Venus

Mercury is the closest planet to the Sun. It has a rocky surface with large craters. Mercury is very hot on the side closest to the Sun.

Venus is the hottest planet. It is even hotter than Mercury because it is covered in clouds which keep heat in. It is the closest planet to Earth.

Mars

Mars is the fourth closest planet to the Sun. It is made from rock and is covered in red dust. For this reason, it is sometimes called the red planet.

Mars is a cold planet. Scientists have been able to send special vehicles called rovers to Mars to take pictures.

Rover

13

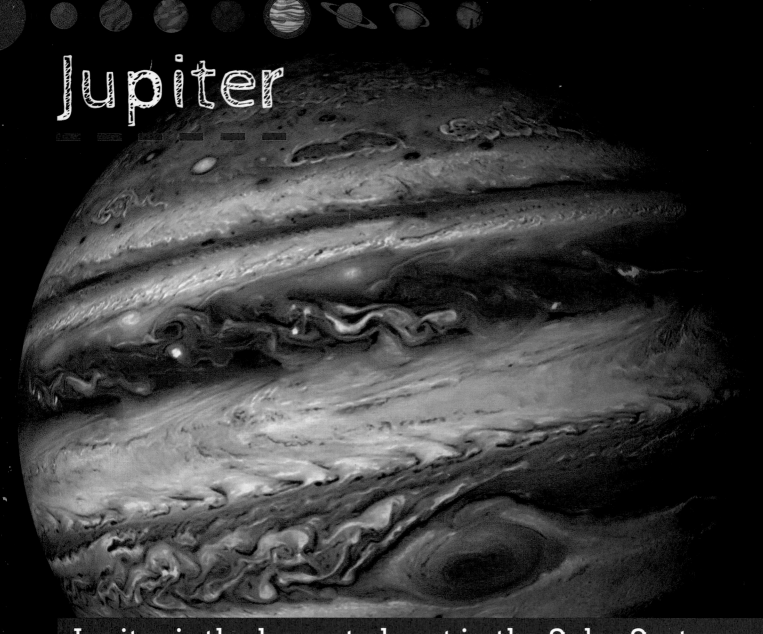

Jupiter

Jupiter is the largest planet in the Solar System. It is a lot bigger than the other planets. Jupiter is mostly made of gas.

Jupiter has over 50 moons which orbit it. Jupiter's largest moon is called Ganymede. Ganymede is bigger than the planet Mercury!

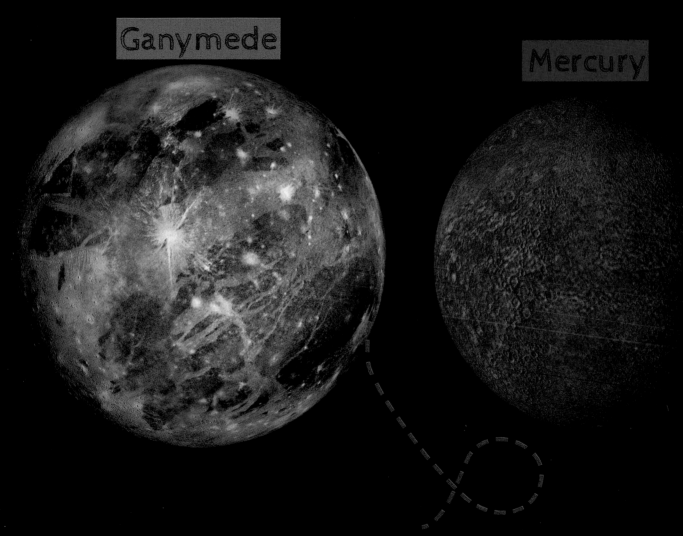

Ganymede

Mercury

Space crafts have successfully visited Jupiter and some of its moons.

Saturn

Saturn is a giant gas planet. It has millions of pieces of rock and ice orbiting it, which makes it look as though Saturn has rings around it.

Saturn has over 50 moons, including the second largest in the whole Solar System. Space crafts have been sent to orbit Saturn and send pictures to scientists.

Uranus and Neptune

Uranus is a large gas planet. It is a cold planet. Uranus spins in a different direction to the other planets which makes it seem as though it has fallen onto its side.

Neptune is the furthest planet from the Sun. Like Uranus, it is a cold gas planet. Only one space craft has visited Neptune.

Dwarf Planets

Dwarf planets are round and orbit the Sun, but they are much smaller than the eight planets. Dwarf planets are even smaller than Earth's moon.

Pluto is a dwarf planet. It used to be one of the main planets, but in 2006 scientists decided it was a dwarf planet.

Earth

Pluto

Many dwarf planets have moons of their own.

21

Perfect Planets!

Venus is the brightest planet in our sky and can sometimes be seen without even using a telescope.

Jupiter is so big that you could fit all the other planets inside it.

Every so often, Mercury can be seen crossing the sun.

Mercury

Neptune has the most stormy weather out of all of the planets.

23

Glossary

asteroids: large rocks which orbit the sun
craters: large holes shaped like bowls
dwarf planets: very small planets
Equator: an imaginary line on planet Earth which shows the hottest part
orbit: move around
telescope: a tool used to make viewing distant objects easier

Index